What a Character!

14 Character-Building Sketches

by

Torry Martin

illenas PUBLISHING COMPANY

KANSAS CITY, MO 64141

Dedication

To William and Verna Martin
For being wonderful parents,
For allowing me my "Torryness"
And for being my best friends

Contents

Acknowledgments 7

Foreword 9

Judge Mental No. 1: A Handy Defense 11

Sergeant Salvation: Episode One: Bible-Thumper 14

Granny Glockenspiel No. 1: Mall Missionary 19

Judge Mental No. 2: Acting Up in Church 23

Sergeant Salvation: Episode Two: Church Calisthenics 26

Judge Mental No. 3: The Bad Place 31

Granny Glockenspiel No. 2: A Very Good Book 34

Judge Mental No. 4: The Problem with Prayer 38

Sergeant Salvation: Episode Three: Off to the Races 41

Judge Mental No. 5: A Rude Awakening 46

Granny Glockenspiel No. 3: Yakkety-Yak 49

Judge Mental No. 6: Solitary Confinement 53

Sergeant Salvation: Episode Four: Earning Your Keep 56

Judge Mental No. 7: Striking Out 61

Acknowledgments

A special thanks . . .

To Robert Austin Browning, my greatest source of encouragement and very best friend.

To Martha Bolton, the true queen of comedy, whose writing, mentoring, and friendship has changed my life completely.

To Pastor Jack Aiken and his lovely wife, Ann, for teaching me so well.

To Ernie Kelly, for his faithfulness, humor, and insight, and for laughing really hard.

To Barbara McBride, for making all of my costumes since I was a kid and being a terrific aunt.

To Monna Shasko for being one of the bravest women I know and showing me what courage is.

To Mae Burmaster and Berenece Martin, two of the greatest grandmothers in the world, I miss you both.

To Scott Fontenot, for being my favorite missionary and a trusted confidant.

To Joe King, for being a great comedy partner and bringing Sergeant Salvation to life.

To Kevin Wines, for being the writer in Comedy College who always cracked me up.

To Tim and Patty Freeman, for their valuable advice and loyal friendship.

To Wendy Cleveland, who has supported my every step.

To Melia Munro, for being my kindred spirit and for praying so faithfully.

To Buddy Buterbaugh, for being my buddy.

To Kim Messer, Stacey Schnarr, and all the groovy people at Lillenas, for making a hippie feel at home. Thanks for making me part of your family.

To Sam, the best dog in the world, and don't you say he isn't.

And to Rusty, the cat I merely tolerate, who is right now walking across my keyboard and bugging me for attention. Yes, Rusty, I acknowledge you.

Foreword

The one question that most people ask me is how I come up with the ideas for the characters I create. The answer is simple . . . I'm twisted. Welcome to the mind of Torry Martin, where everything is analyzed and exaggerated, then shaken and stirred until nothing is as it seems. While most of you will be just visiting, please keep in mind that I live here and it even scares me.

Hopefully this book will enlighten others in a nonthreatening manner to the following facts:

- Jesus is more concerned with a person's heart than He is with the person's appearance.
- The character of a ministry is more important than the methodology.
- Believers are to be united in love, not divided by taste.
- Humor is a good thing.

I have created three characters that best help me demonstrate the importance of these concepts, and you will be meeting them shortly, but first I'd like to take this opportunity to explain their origins.

Judge Mental: The concept for Judge Mental came to me one day while sharing a pot of coffee with my friend Ernie. We were sitting and sipping while complaining to each other about how unfairly we were often judged by others, but of course we were passing our own judgments in the process. Suddenly we realized we needed to get the plank out of our own eyes and focus on our own flaws instead. We also realized that this would make a great character for a series onstage or on the radio, and so Judge Mental was born. Think of Boss Hogg from *The Dukes of Hazard,* and then place that character in a courtroom and you'll get the picture. Judge Mental rules with an iron gavel in the Court of Popular Opinion where his trusty sidekick Bobby Ray the bailiff accompanies him. The judge has an uncanny ability to rule on all aspects of church ministry and behavior and considers himself to be the ultimate authority on any given subject. As much as I hate to admit it, I seem to have some of the judge's characteristics in myself and as soon as I finish straightening up everyone else in the Kingdom I'll set to work on fixing that.

Granny Glockenspiel: I was asked to create a radio character for a local Christian radio station and quickly decided that I didn't want to stay within the typical bounds of safety for what a Christian character should be. Granny was going to have some flaws, she was going to be eccentric, and she was going to have fun in her Christian walk. In my mind she is in her late 60s, but in her mind she is ageless. Though we often disagree on things, Granny is probably more a part of my own personality than any other character I have created. We both prefer motorcycles to cars, dogs to cats, and godliness to religion. We both blunder through life and question everything while saying whatever we want whenever we like. This also explains why we both don't have many friends.

Sergeant Salvation: My former comedy partner Joe King did a great drill sergeant's voice, and I wanted to incorporate it as a character in one of our shows. I developed this character for him, and he quickly became an audience favorite. Sergeant Salvation is as religious and legalistic as they come. He teaches a class for new believers on the basics of Christianity, and he takes his job very seriously. He's bossy, demanding, temperamental, direct, abrupt, rude, and skilled in the art of manipulation. He also has a heart that can pull at him on occasion. I think every church has at least one Sergeant Salvation in attendance, you might even recognize him in yourself, in which case . . . I salute you.

I hope you will have as much fun with these characters as I've had with them myself. They are all bold, exaggerated, and unique in their perspectives. But what I hope for most is that you will love them in spite of their many flaws just as Jesus loves us in spite of ours.

JUDGE MENTAL NO. 1
A Handy Defense

Characters:
> JUDGE MENTAL
> EMILY FENMORE
> BAILIFF (BOBBY RAY)

Setting: Courtroom

Props: Gavel

Costumes: JUDGE wears a black robe (graduation gown). BAILIFF wears tan pants and shirt with a badge. EMILY is wearing a very bright, distracting dress.

(BAILIFF *enters and stands at attention with hands behind him.*)

BAILIFF *(to congregation):* All rise! *(If they don't rise, BAILIFF will persist until they do!)* The Court of Popular Opinion is now in session. The Honorable Judge Mental is now presiding. (BAILIFF *stands still;* JUDGE *enters.*)

JUDGE *(sits and shuffles through papers on desk; looks at congregation and then hits gavel):* You may be seated. Docket No. 53, *The Church v. Emily Fenmore.* Is the defendant present?

EMILY *(seated in the congregation; she rises):* Yes, your Honor.

JUDGE: The defendant will please approach the bench and be seated. (EMILY *does so.*) I've got a complaint against you that says you've been raising a ruckus with the use of your hands during worship service. Is this true?

EMILY: Raising a ruckus?

JUDGE: That's right.

EMILY: With my hands?

JUDGE: Right again. Now you string those two thoughts together and take as long as you want.

EMILY: Raising a ruckus with my hands?

JUDGE: Oooieee. You're quicker than I thought.

EMILY: Judge, I don't know what you're talking about.

JUDGE *(fed up and condescending):* I'm talking about . . . raising *(raises hands ener-*

11

getically) . . . a ruckus . . . *(claps hands together a few times loudly)* . . . with your haaaaaands! *(Waves hands dramatically at her)*

EMILY: Oh.

JUDGE: Now do you know what I'm talking about?

EMILY: Well, I have clapped my hands a few times during the fast songs, and I've also lifted them in praise to God on occasion, but I most certainly have not raised a ruckus.

JUDGE: Dear lady, raising your hands *is* raising a ruckus! It's not only distracting but also qualifies you as being a spiritual stuck-up!

EMILY: A spiritual stuck-up?

JUDGE: Yeah! You think you're better than all them people who ain't waving their hands in the air!

EMILY: Your Honor, I simply became moved by the song we were singing, and I put my hymnal down so I could lift my hands to God. It wasn't my intention to distract anyone or to appear stuck-up.

JUDGE: I'll be the one to tell ya what your intentions are! Do you know why we use the hymnal during services, Miss Fenmore?

EMILY: Why, I suppose it's to be able to read the lyrics to the song we're singing.

JUDGE: That is only partially correct. There is a twofold reason for using the hymnal. The other reason is to keep your hands busy holding something so they aren't flopping around all over the place distracting others.

EMILY: That's ridiculous.

JUDGE *(angry):* I'll be the one in this courtroom who decides what ridiculous is, and I'll start with that dress you have on!

EMILY *(looks at her clothes):* What's wrong with it? I paid good money for this!

JUDGE: I'm sorry, Ma'am. Could you speak a little louder, please? I can barely hear you over your outfit.

EMILY *(indignant):* Well! I've never been so insulted in my life!

JUDGE: And neither have my eyes. *(A beat)* You just have to have attention on yourself no matter where you go or what you do, don't ya? But that's beside the point. Let's get back to these charges. *(Looks at papers on his desk)* Now, what can you tell me about this hand-*clapping* nonsense of yours?

EMILY: I was just trying to make a joyful noise unto the Lord, like the Bible says.

JUDGE: Clapping ain't joyful, it's just noise!

EMILY: I just thought . . .

JUDGE: Who asked you to think? Just because one specific individual takes it into her mind that something is a joyful noise—that don't necessarily make it so! Approach the bench, please. Let me show ya what I mean. Get right up here where I can see you eye to eye. Thank you, now look at me . . . is ya looking?

EMILY: Yes.

JUDGE *(raspberries her):* Pfffffllllt. Is that a joyful noise?

EMILY: Definitely not.

JUDGE: Huh, well I say it is! How 'bout next Sunday we all just sing "Amazing Grace" like this, join me, Bobby Ray. *(They both raspberry "Amazing Grace.")* All right, Bobby Ray, you continue. Now, Miss Fenmore, would you say that is joyful or just distracting?

EMILY *(dryly):* Definitely distracting.

JUDGE: And so is that hand-raising, hand-clapping, hand-me-down hippie behavior you was doing at church. Bobby Ray, stop!

BAILIFF *(lisping):* Thangs, my thongue wath goin' numb.

JUDGE: Well, now that I have successfully proven my point, let's proceed with the sentencing.

EMILY: Wait a second! Shouldn't I be judged by a jury of my peers?

(JUDGE and BAILIFF look at each other and start laughing.)

JUDGE *(to BAILIFF)*: Did ya hear that, Bobby Ray?

BAILIFF *(wiping eyes and still laughing):* I sure did, Judge. That were funny.

JUDGE: Madam, may I remind you that this here is a *church* courtroom? We can't git 12 people around here to agree on nuttin'! I hereby rule Miss Emily Fenmore guilty of raising a ruckus and hereby sentence her to one year of children's church duties! *(Slams gavel)*

EMILY: Children's church?

JUDGE: Yeah, you want to play with your hands so much, then you can do it playing patty-cake. Please see the bailiff. Court's adjourned! *(Chuckling to himself as he exits)* Jury? That's a good one.

(JUDGE exits and BAILIFF escorts EMILY out.)

SERGEANT SALVATION
Episode One: Bible-Thumper

Characters:

> HEATHER: *A smart girl who was raised in church but just recently came to the Lord*
> TOM: *A brand-new Christian but a little apprehensive*
> SARGE: *Drill sergeant intent on laying down the laws of the church to newcomers*

Setting: A classroom set up with six folding chairs

Props: Pocket Bible for TOM and a very large "Bible" for SARGE (SARGE's "Bible" can be made out of a large piece of foam covered with painted cardboard for a book jacket.)

(TOM *is seated center stage with an empty chair beside him. He looks around nervously, then opens his pocket Bible and reads it silently.* HEATHER *walks up behind him unnoticed. She leans forward and says:*)

HEATHER: Hi!

TOM *(reacts and jumps up, startled):* Whoa! You scared me.

HEATHER: Sorry, I didn't have time to fix my hair this morning.

TOM *(laughs):* No, I mean I wasn't expecting anyone to sneak up on me like that.

HEATHER: I was just having some fun. My name's Heather. *(She extends her hand.)*

TOM: Hi, I'm Tom. *(They shake hands.)* Are you here for the class?

HEATHER *(sitting):* Yep, the bulletin said it's mandatory that all baby Christians attend, so here I am.

TOM *(sitting):* Well, good! I'm glad I'm not alone anymore. I was getting a little nervous.

HEATHER: Nervous? *(She laughs.)* I never would have guessed.

TOM: It's the classroom. I feel like I'm going to be tested or something.

HEATHER: Naw, I'm sure the instructor will be like really, really nice and stuff. I mean, after all, he is a Christian, right?

SARGE *(yells while entering at a rapid pace):* Aaaaaaaaaattention!

TOM *(pause):* Whoa!

SARGE: I want all new baby Christians in formation and toeing the line! *Now!* Move, move, move, and move! *(They both jump up and stand in front of* SARGE.*)* Welcome to Basic Christianity Boot Camp. My name is Sergeant Salvation, and for the next few weeks I'll be your authority figure, your mentor, and your drill instructor!

BOTH *(look at each other):* Uh-oh.

SARGE: And for some of you, I'll be your worst nightmare!

TOM: Uh, that would be me, over here, Sir.

HEATHER *(to* TOM*):* Must be another victim of too much caffeine!

(Both give a nervous laugh.)

SARGE: What's that you said, girlie?

HEATHER: I said, make me a lean, mean Christian machine!

SARGE: That's what I like to hear, and that's exactly what I'm gonna do. It's my job to train new recruits, and I take pride in doing it. Now, it's gonna be hard, it's gonna be fast, and it's gonna be done correctly. Most folks can't cut it and go AWOL before basic training is even completed.

TOM: What does AWOL mean?

SARGE: Another wimp out loser. Is that what you want to be, Son, another wimp out loser? Is it? Answer me!

TOM: No!

SARGE: No what?

TOM: No, Sir!

SARGE: Good, then let's get started.

HEATHER: Umm . . . I have a few questions before we get started, Sir.

SARGE: Questions? Questions? You are not here to question but to learn! What's that you're holding in your hand, Boy?

TOM: This? Oh, it's just a pocket Bible.

SARGE: A pocket Bible? That there's a concealed weapon! Lesson one: Ain't nobody gonna notice a dinky old Bible that size! We want our weapons out in the open so everyone can see them and be intimidated! If you're gonna be in the Lord's army, you gotta learn to make your weapon noticeable! Like this one! *(Holds up a big Bible)*

HEATHER: Whoa, check out the size of that! Wow!

TOM: Hey, um, excuse me, Sarge, but I don't get it. How is the Bible supposed to be used as a weapon?

SARGE (*singsong mockery imitation of* TOM): How is the Bible used as a weapon? How is the Bible used as a weapon? You really are baby Christians, aren't you? Don't you know it's a war out there? If someone comes up to you and disagrees about what the Bible says, you gotta be ready to use your weapon.

HEATHER: Oh, you mean to quote scriptures to them and have a ready answer.

SARGE: No, that's not what I mean! Son, get up here so we can give the little lady a demonstration. (*He grabs* TOM *by the ear and pulls him forward.*)

TOM: Ow, ow, ow, ow!

SARGE: Now, let's pretend I'm a Christian and you're a non-Christian and you are challenging me on what I believe. Ya think you can do that, Son?

TOM (*scared and rubbing ear):* Yes, Sir.

SARGE: Good, then let's begin! (*Clears throat*) Hi! I'm a Christian!

TOM (*intimidated):* Hi, I'm a non-Christian and I'm going to challenge you on what you believe, Sir.

(SARGE *gives a quick three-punch by hitting him in gut with Bible.* TOM *doubles over, and* SARGE *hits him on the back of head with Bible and finishes him off by hitting him on the back with Bible.* TOM *drops to the floor.* SARGE *blows the end of his Bible off.*)

SARGE (*puts foot on* TOM's *back proudly):* And that there is how we use our Bibles as a weapon, more commonly known in lay terms as Bible-thumping! Now, get up and get back in line!

HEATHER (*to* TOM): Are you all right?

TOM: Yeah, I think so.

HEATHER: That wasn't very nice, Sarge.

SARGE: Nice? Who cares about being nice? I'm talking about being Christian. Now who can tell me what lesson two is?

TOM: How to recover from a blow to the head?

SARGE: No! (*Thumps* TOM *on the head with his Bible again*) Lesson two is, you must never challenge your drill instructor. Remember that. And lesson three is, the King James Version is not only the most reliable make of the Bible but also the only make you will be allowed to carry.

HEATHER: Just a second, Sarge. I hate to correct you or anything, but I read that according to scholars and theologians that the *New American Standard* is the best word-for-word translation available and . . .

SARGE: Hold it right there, Private, what was lesson number two? (SARGE *pauses while* HEATHER *thinks.*) Tom, why don't you help her out?

TOM: Never challenge your drill instructor?

SARGE: Very good! Now, would you say Heather here was challenging me?

TOM: Well, I guess so . . . sorta . . .

(SARGE *does three thumps on* TOM *again; he lands on floor in a heap.*)

TOM: Hey! What'd ya do that for? She's the one who challenged you.

SARGE: Yes, but you ought to know better than to be the bearer of bad news!

TOM *(still on the floor):* I think I'll just stay down here.

HEATHER *(interrupting):* Umm . . . excuse me, Sarge, but I think you owe Tom an apology.

SARGE: An apology? For what?

HEATHER: Well, for breaking one of the greatest commandments of all, for starters.

SARGE: Listen here, Missy, I ain't never broken a commandment in my entire military career.

HEATHER: What about, "You shall love your neighbor as yourself"?

SARGE: Well . . . uh . . .

HEATHER: It's in the Bible.

SARGE: King James Version?

HEATHER: I think so.

SARGE: Tell me this, Private. How do you know so much about the Bible if you're just a baby Christian?

HEATHER: I was raised in the church, but I only recently accepted the Lord, Sir.

SARGE *(pauses):* Huh, talk about slow learners. The fact remains that I'm teaching this boy here about self-defense, and if that ain't love, I don't know what is.

TOM *(from floor):* Could you just love me a little less then?

SARGE: All right, sissy boy, you can get back up now. I'll try to lighten up on ya a little.

TOM: Thanks.

SARGE *(noticing* HEATHER *is being quiet):* Now what's the matter with you?

HEATHER: I was just thinking that it shouldn't matter what version of the Bible people read as long as they're reading it. And your insistence on using the King James Version sounds a little legalistic.

SARGE: Legalistic?

TOM: Uh-oh. (TOM *lies back down.*)

HEATHER: You do know what that means, right?

SARGE: Umm . . . we'll need to get back to that next week after I look it up, I mean after I look you up. OK, I think that's just about enough for today. So what'd we learn?

HEATHER: Carry a big Bible.

TOM: And wear a helmet.

SARGE: Good! Class dismissed.

TOM: Thanks, Sarge.

HEATHER (*to* SARGE): See ya next week. (*Walking out with* TOM) Can I drop you off anywhere?

TOM (*rubbing head):* Mercy Hospital.

(*Both exit.*)

SARGE: Legalistic? Now where's that dictionary? (*Looks at his Bible and realizes it's actually a dictionary)* Oops. (*Looking it up in dictionary while exiting)* Let's see . . . leeward . . . leeway . . . left brained . . . leftovers . . . left wing . . . legalese . . . (*He exits.*)

GRANNY GLOCKENSPIEL NO. 1
Mall Missionary

Characters:
GRANNY GLOCKENSPIEL
LAURA

Setting: A peaceful rest bench in a local mall

Props: Exercise bag, motorcycle helmet

Costumes: GRANNY: Anything leopard-print, especially jumpsuits or a sweat suit with rhinestones, gaudy jewelry, spandex, big scarves, really big hair, red nails, and always wears white tennis shoes. Use body padding to comical effect. LAURA: Contemporary clothing.

GRANNY: Whew! I am one tired Granny. Mind if I take a load off?

LAURA *(scooting over):* Sure, go ahead.

GRANNY *(sits down):* Thanks. I've been walking the mall all morning.

LAURA: That's what I'm supposed to be doing.

GRANNY: Taking a break, huh? How many laps did you do?

LAURA: Well, none yet.

GRANNY: Just checking out the competition?

LAURA *(hesitant):* No, I . . . I . . . I seem to have lost my motivation, I guess. *(Pause)* Look, I don't really want to bother you with my problems.

GRANNY: Oh, you're not bothering me at all. Here, let me give you my card. *(Pulls business card out of her pocket and hands it to* LAURA*)*

LAURA *(reading):* Granny Glockenspiel, Mall Missionary. *(A beat)* You're a Christian?

GRANNY: That's right, and the mall is my mission field. You're sitting on my bench, you know.

LAURA: Your bench? Oh, I'm sorry; I didn't know. *(Starts to get up)*

GRANNY: No, sit, sit. You're supposed to be here.

LAURA: I am?

GRANNY: Yep. This is the bench I always rest on when I do my walking. *(Proudly)* I ask God every day to take whoever He wants me to talk to and make them sit right here. *(Patting seat)*

LAURA: That's nice.

GRANNY: Yep, and today it's you. So what's your name?

LAURA: I'm Laura.

GRANNY: OK, Laura, what can I help you with?

LAURA: Help me? But I'm already a Christian.

GRANNY *(interrupting):* So? Christians have problems, too, ya know.

LAURA: They do? I mean . . . do you have problems?

GRANNY: You betcha, I do.

LAURA: Like what?

GRANNY: Like right now somebody is sitting on my side of the bench.

LAURA: Oh! I'm sorry! (LAURA *and* GRANNY *stand up and switch seats.)* Better?

GRANNY: Much! Well, my problem's solved, so let's work on yours.

LAURA: My problem? Oh it's nothing, really. It's just that I get discouraged so easily.

GRANNY: Discouraged?

LAURA: Like, take this morning for instance. I woke up ready to start fresh at something new, like exercising, ya know? Everything was going great, and I was determined to be productive, but then . . .

GRANNY: But then what?

LAURA: But then on my way here I got stuck behind this guy on a motorcycle who was put-putting along at 30 miles an hour in the fast lane, and he wouldn't get out of my way!

GRANNY: He put you in a bad mood, eh?

LAURA: I'll say. My positive attitude went right out the window along with the fist I was furiously shaking at the guy.

GRANNY: Uh-oh.

LAURA: I tried honking at him, but that didn't work because he couldn't hear me through his helmet, right? Then I tried waving at him.

GRANNY: Did it get his attention?

LAURA: I think so. He waved back.

GRANNY: You should have just passed him.

LAURA: I tried, but he turned his left-hand blinker on like he was gonna turn, so I didn't.

GRANNY: You didn't?

LAURA: Nope and neither did he. Turn, that is. He just kept his blinker on for the next seven miles while continuing to drive completely oblivious.

GRANNY: Boy, I don't blame you for being discouraged. Something like that would have sent me off my rocker, too, let me tell ya.

LAURA: The worst part is . . . well . . . you should have heard the things that were coming out of my mouth while I was following him.

GRANNY: Well, Laura, I think I'm glad that I didn't.

LAURA: Oh, I was so angry! I hardly felt like a Christian at all.

GRANNY: So what's that got to do with you getting some exercise?

LAURA: I just feel like I've let God down with my behavior, so I've lost my motivation to do anything.

GRANNY: Oh, boohoo-hoo, what a bunch of rubbish.

LAURA: I beg your pardon?

GRANNY *(to herself):* God save me from whiny Christians. *(To* LAURA*)* Ya can't give up just because ya lost your temper. Being a Christian is supposed to be difficult.

LAURA: It is?

GRANNY: Well, if not there'd be more scriptures about skipping and sailing through the Christian life and less scriptures about striving and struggling through it.

LAURA: Then why do I feel like such a failure?

GRANNY: Who knows? Maybe ya like it. Listen, would it help if I told you that I lost my temper myself this morning?

LAURA: You did?

GRANNY: Yep and over the same thing as you almost.

LAURA: What happened?

GRANNY: Oh, some guy tailgated me the whole way here. I slowed down for him to pass, but he preferred to stay behind and harass me instead.

LAURA: I don't even know how some people got their licenses.

GRANNY: The point is that even though I was upset about it, I just shrugged it off and got to the business of the day. And if you're smart, you'll do the same.

LAURA: It's too late to start walking now, though; the mall's about to open.

GRANNY: Well, then why don't you come to breakfast with me where we can plan out your exercise schedule for tomorrow and get ya back on track?

LAURA: That would be wonderful!

GRANNY: Do you know where Billy-Bob's Breakfast Buffet is?

LAURA: No, not really.

GRANNY (standing): Don't worry about it, then, and just follow me.

LAURA: You've got it.

GRANNY: Just don't follow too closely, if ya know what I mean.

LAURA: No tailgating allowed. (Laughs) I'll meet you out front.

GRANNY: Okeydokey, Sweetie. I won't be hard to miss. (Brings motorcycle helmet out of exercise bag) I'll be the one in the helmet.

LAURA (realizing): You drive . . . a motorcycle?

GRANNY: Of course!

LAURA: A bright red motorcycle with orange flames painted on it?

GRANNY: It's a beauty! I have to get it over to the shop, though. My left-hand blinker was busted the whole way here. See ya outside, Sweetie. (She exits through congregation energetically. LAURA stays in shock center stage.)

LAURA: I knew God worked in mysterious ways, but this is almost too weird! (She exits.)

JUDGE MENTAL NO. 2
Acting Up in Church

Characters:
> Judge Mental
> Jimmy Butler: *youth pastor*
> Bailiff (Bobby Ray)

Setting: Courtroom

Props: Gavel

Costumes: Judge wears a black robe (graduation gown). Bailiff wears tan pants and shirt with a badge. Jimmy is dressed in contemporary clothing.

(NOTE: Whenever Judge or Bailiff use the word *drama,* they pronounce it in a way that rhymes with "bama" as in AlaBAMA.)

(Bailiff *enters and stands at attention with hands behind him.*)

Bailiff *(to congregation):* All rise! (*If they don't rise,* Bailiff *will persist until they do!*) The Court of Popular Opinion is now in session. The Honorable Judge Mental is now presiding. (Bailiff *stands still;* Judge *enters.*)

Judge *(sits and shuffles through papers on desk; looks at congregation and then hits gavel):* You may be seated. Docket No. 54, *The Church v. Pastor Jimmy Butler.* Is the defendant present?

Jimmy *(seated in the congregation, he rises):* Yes, your Honor.

Judge: The defendant will please approach the bench and be seated. (Jimmy *does so.*) It says here that you took it into your puny little youth pastor mind to incorporate a creative illustration of the pastor's sermon last Sunday morning. Just what exactly does the term *creative illustration* mean?

Jimmy: It was a drama to illustrate the sermon, Sir.

Judge: "Dramma?" "Dramma?" "Dramma" in the church? What were you thinking, Sonny?

Jimmy: Well, I went to a youth seminar and . . .

Judge *(interrupting):* A what?

Jimmy: A youth seminar, you know, a seminar for youth leaders.

Judge: Did you hear that, Bailiff? A seminar.

Bailiff: Seminar?

JUDGE: Says he learned about "dramma."

BAILIFF: "Dramma?"

JUDGE: Exactly! So tell us, Mr. Hoity-Toity Seminar-Going Youth Pastor, just what exactly does "dramma" have to do with church?

BAILIFF: Yeah, tell us!

JIMMY: Well, I learned that this is the visual age we are living in . . .

JUDGE (interrupts with a groan): Uuuuhhhh . . .

JIMMY: And that people learn better if they can actually see a dramatic presentation that helps show the point the pastor is trying to make.

JUDGE: So we got us a regular Steven Spielberg, huh? Well, listen, Mr. Hollywood . . .

BAILIFF (repeating JUDGE): Yeah, Mr. Hollywood.

JUDGE: "Dramma" belongs in the theatre, the theatre belongs on Broadway, Broadway belongs in New York City, and every good Christian knows that New York City belongs to the devil. Let me make this easier for your simple youth pastor mind . . . D-"Dramma" . . . D-Demons, D-Devil! Got it?

JIMMY: Not really.

JUDGE: Well, then, let me put it in terms that your actor's mind can understand. Remember that movie *Titanic*?

JIMMY: Yes.

JUDGE: And you know Leonardo DiCaprio?

JIMMY: Yeah. He was the hero.

JUDGE: That's right, and that's me. Now I want you to just think of yourself as that other main character, the *Titanic* itself, 'cuz you're just a great big ship that's going down!

JIMMY: You do know that if we stuck to the script, your character would be going down with me, right?

JUDGE: Nah-uh. 'Cause, see, Leonardo was playing an imaginary character. But the *Titanic*? Now that was real, and so is this courtroom. Now do you see what I mean? "Dramma" no more belongs in the church than Leonardo belonged in that movie.

JIMMY: Aren't you stretching that analogy a little bit?

JUDGE: As a pastor, I think you'd be used to that.

JIMMY: I'm just having some difficulty in following your thought process.

JUDGE: Bobby Ray, are you having any problems following my thought process?

BAILIFF: Nope.

JUDGE: Let's do a little test to make sure. What's two plus two?

BAILIFF: Twenty-two?

JUDGE: That's right, we're fine. *(To* JIMMY*)* Now, I don't want you getting the opinion that I don't like theatre. I enjoy the theatre very much and have even participated in a few productions myself.

JIMMY: You're an actor? Wow, I'm impressed.

JUDGE: You should be. I'll have you know I played Hamlette.

JIMMY: As in Shakespeare's masterpiece *Hamlet*?

JUDGE: No, as in Mother Goose's masterpiece "The Three Little Pigs." There was Piglette and Omelette and then there was little Hamlette. That was me, I was the youngest. It was grade school, but it was funny.

JIMMY *(looking around quickly):* Is there a camera around here?

JUDGE: No, why, ya want a picture of your last day as a free man?

JIMMY: No, I was looking for Alan Funt.

JUDGE: Sounds to me like you are making a mockery of my courtroom.

JIMMY: You don't need me for that.

JUDGE: My point exactly. Now let's conclude our little daytime "dramma" and proceed with the sentencing.

JIMMY: Sentencing? Fine, but before you do that, I'd like to go on record as saying you have exhibited the most childish behavior for a judge that I've ever seen.

JUDGE: Childish behavior? Childish behavior? *(Taunting like a kid)* Well, I'm rubber and you're glue, what bounces off me sticks on you! *(Back to his normal angry self)* OK, Mr. Actor Man! I find you guilty as charged and hereby sentence you to three months of nursery duty!

JIMMY: Nursery duty?

JUDGE: Yep, and that's where you'll find out what *childish behavior* really is. Since you like to act so much, let's see how well you do in playing the role of mama! Court's adjourned! Bailiff, take him away! *(Muttering to himself)* "Dramma" in a church. What'll be next? Drums?

(JUDGE *exits and* BAILIFF *escorts* JIMMY *offstage.*)

SERGEANT SALVATION
Episode Two: Church Calisthenics

Characters:
    SARGE
    TOM
    HEATHER

Setting: Church sanctuary

Props: Pew, piano rollers for pew, camouflage tarp or blanket

Costumes: Sergeant uniform for SARGE and casual clothing for TOM and
    HEATHER

(TOM *and* HEATHER *enter together. Both stop in the middle of the platform and look
around curiously.)*

TOM: Hey . . . does something seem not right in here?

HEATHER: Where'd all the chairs go?

TOM: Ya can't have a class without chairs. Where are we supposed to sit?

HEATHER: Maybe they moved the class or something and just didn't tell us.

TOM: Nope, it said in the bulletin that all classes for baby Christians would be
    held permanently in the nursery.

HEATHER: Let's just sit on the floor then. After all, Sarge did say that as baby
    Christians we're going to have to learn to crawl before we learn to walk.
    (She sits.)

TOM: Yeah, but I didn't think he meant it literally. *(Pause)* Oh well. (TOM *sits on
floor next to* HEATHER.) So what's new?

HEATHER *(looking at floor carefully):* Definitely not the shag carpeting.

TOM *(laughs):* Did Sarge happen to mention to you what he was going to be
    talking about this week?

HEATHER: Nope, apparently it's top secret. Very hush-hush.

SARGE *(yells while entering at a rapid pace):* Aaaaaaaaaattention! I want all new
    baby Christians in formation and toeing the line! *Now!* Move, move,
    move, and move! *(They both jump up and stand in front of* SARGE.) Welcome
    to Basic Christianity Boot Camp. My name is Sergeant Salvation, and for

the next few weeks I'll be your authority figure, your mentor, your drill instructor, and for some of you, I'll be your worst nightmare.

TOM *(sarcastic):* Wow, dreams really do come true.

SARGE: What's that you said, Boy?

TOM: I said you're a Christian dream come true, Sir!

SARGE: And don't you forget it. All right, my baby Christians, I got something over here I want you to see! *(Starts to roll in a pew that is on rollers and hidden under a camouflage tarp)* This here is the most important top secret piece of equipment within the church structure!

HEATHER: The most important piece of equipment in the whole church?

SARGE: That's right!

TOM: Hmm . . . is it an espresso bar?

SARGE: No!

HEATHER: A bingo machine?

SARGE: No!

TOM: Oooooh, maybe it's a tank!

SARGE: Are you on drugs, Boy? What on earth would a tank be doing in a church?

HEATHER: Well, it could be a big portable baptismal tank!

TOM *(excitedly):* Yeah, a great big portable baptismal tank! *(Laughs)* Coming soon to a revival near you!

SARGE: Ha-ha, you're a pretty funny boy, aren't ya?

TOM: Well, my friends all . . .

SARGE: Shut yer yap! Now concealed beneath this shroud of excellence is an item you will both become familiar with! I want you to know it, love it, and befriend it . . . because this here is what we most commonly refer to as . . . the all-powerful, all-encompassing, and almighty . . . *(pause and unveils it)* . . .

HEATHER: Bus bench?

SARGE: No! That's not a bus bench! It's a pew!

TOM: A pew?

SARGE *(whistles):* Yesiree! The pew! It's a beaut, isn't it? *(Pause)* What's the matter, Boy? Cat got yer tongue? Ain't ya never seen a pew before?

TOM: No, Sir, I've only smelt a pew before, but I never actually saw one. *(Laughs)*

SARGE: Is that a stinky joke? I don't cotton to no stinky jokes! Now help me get this pew down off its holy rollers and get it situated where I can show ya how it's used! *(They lift the pew off the rollers and set it on the ground.)* Attention! (TOM *and* HEATHER *snap to attention and* SARGE *starts to pace.)* This magnificent piece of man-made heavy wooden furniture is to be treated with the utmost respect! Heather! Do you know why?

HEATHER: Well, no, Sir, but I imagine it's because . . .

SARGE *(interrupting):* Because this here piece of machinery is gonna become a part of you! And I mean that literally! Now a lot of people like to have their pews softly padded . . .

TOM: Hey! That's a cool idea.

SARGE: No it is not! And some churches are even as sacrilegious as to get rid of the pew altogether and use comfortable chairs instead . . .

HEATHER: Oh, that sounds nice.

SARGE: But I say nah-uh! I won't have none of that! No sir! Now sit! *(Both sit on pew now.)* Now, who can tell me what the first thing is ya do when ya sit in your pew?

HEATHER *(raises her hand):* Oh, I know! Pick me! Pick me!

SARGE *(as if he is trying to choose between several people trying to answer):* Hmmm . . . hmmm. Uh, Heather?

HEATHER: Relax and meditate in the house of God?

SARGE: No! The first thing ya do when ya get in yer pew is to . . . *(Plops down between them and scoots his bottom around)* Shine with your behind! Shine with your behind! *(Stands back up)* This here equipment needs to be kept up and polished, so when you sit on it your first duty is to . . . what?

BOTH *(both scoot their bottoms around enthusiastically):* Shine with our behinds! Shine with our behinds!

SARGE: Now, idn't that fun? *(Blows whistle)* Now we're gonna play a little game.

HEATHER: I like games!

SARGE: Hush up, nobody cares what ya like! This here game is sort of a rendition of Simon says . . . only we call it Pastor says. . . . Ready?

BOTH: Ready, Sir!

SARGE *(blows whistle):* Let the games begin! *(Paces and tries to catch them messing up)* Pastor says . . . stand up for the reading of the Word!

(They stand.)

SARGE: Pastor says . . . sit down for the announcements.

(They sit.)

SARGE: Pastor says . . . stand up to sing a song from the hymnal!

(They stand.)

SARGE: Pastor says . . . sit down for the choir's special number!

(They sit.)

SARGE: Pastor says . . . stand up and greet yer neighbor!

(They stand.)

SARGE: Sit down!

(They sit.)

SARGE: What are you doing?

BOTH: Sitting down.

SARGE: Did Pastor say?

BOTH: Oops.

SARGE: Up, up, up, up! *(They both jump up.)* Nobody but nobody stands up or sits down until Pastor says! *Now* Pastor says . . . sit down!

(They sit.)

SARGE: Pastor says . . . stand up for prayer!

(They stand.)

SARGE: Pastor says . . . sit down for the offering.

TOM *(exasperated)*: Sit down, stand up, sit down, stand up! Is this church or an aerobics class?

SARGE: What's that, Boy?

HEATHER: I think what Tom is trying to say is that we're not in church to compete with our neighbors about whose pew is shinier or for a "game" of who can sit down and stand up the fastest. We're here to learn more about God.

SARGE: Is that what you were saying, Son?

TOM: No, I just don't like exercise.

HEATHER: Tom!

Tom: OK. And I agree with what she said.

Sarge: Hmmm . . . Is that so? Teaming up, are ya? Well, it appears that I've been outvoted then . . . *(looks at watch)* and lookie here, we're out of time. *(Turns his back to them)* Class dismissed. *(Lowers head sadly)*

Heather *(apologetically):* Sarge, we aren't teaming up on . . .

Sarge: I said, dismissed!

Tom: Come on, Heather, let's go before he changes his mind.

Heather: See ya next week, Sarge.

Sarge *(looks up after they exit and waxes philosophical to audience):* You know, maybe they're right. Maybe church isn't a game. Maybe that makes me feel compelled to change my whole philosophy. Maybe something deep inside me is stirring up for the very first time. *(Lengthy pause, as if considering what he has said)* Naaaah! Maybe I just don't like being outvoted. Speaking of which . . . *(looks at watch again),* as chairman of the church board, I'd better get to that meeting for our voting tonight. After all, I want to get home in time for the *Gomer Pyle* marathon. *(Laughs to himself)* That Gomer.

JUDGE MENTAL NO. 3
The Bad Place

Characters:
> JUDGE MENTAL
> STAN MORRISON: *pastor*
> BAILIFF (BOBBY RAY)

Setting: Courtroom

Props: Gavel

Costumes: JUDGE wears a black robe (graduation gown). BAILIFF wears tan pants and shirt with a badge. STAN is dressed in contemporary clothing.

(BAILIFF *enters and stands at attention with hands behind him.*)

BAILIFF *(to congregation):* All rise! *(If they don't rise, BAILIFF will persist until they do!)* The Court of Popular Opinion is now in session. The Honorable Judge Mental is now presiding. (BAILIFF *stands still;* JUDGE *enters.*)

JUDGE *(sits and shuffles through papers on desk; looks at congregation and then hits gavel):* You may be seated. Docket No. 55, *The Church v. Pastor Stan Morrison.* Is the defendant present?

STAN *(seated in the congregation, he rises):* Yes, your Honor.

JUDGE: The defendant will please approach the bench and be seated. (STAN *does so.*) It says here that you preached a sermon that insinuated some of the people in your congregation wouldn't be going to heaven if they didn't change their ways.

STAN: I did mention that some people would have to make a decision to repent of their sins or they would be facing eternal damnation in hell.

(JUDGE *and* BAILIFF *both gasp in unison.*)

JUDGE: Bobby Ray, it appears that Pastor here is a potty-mouth.

BAILIFF *(to* STAN*):* Potty-mouth!

STAN: Potty-mouth?

JUDGE: Potty-mouth!

STAN: Preaching about the dangers of falling into the pit of . . . *(thinking)*

JUDGE *(interrupting):* You'd better watch it right there!

STAN: Fine, let me rephrase. *(Sighs)* Preaching about the dangers of falling into the pits of the bad place does not make me a potty-mouth.

JUDGE: I'm the judge, and I say it does. But tell me this, why on earth would you choose to preach on the bad place anyway?

STAN: My job as a pastor is to care for my sheep, and I believe that includes informing them of the reality of . . . the bad place.

JUDGE: Oh, you try to make it sound so noble when you explain it like that, but you are way out of line on this one. You see, the bad place is hot, and hot is uncomfortable, and there's one thing no one wants to feel in church and that's uncomfortable.

STAN: What is wrong with people feeling uncomfortable in church? Conviction is good for the soul.

JUDGE: Don't talk to me about conviction! My whole career is about conviction! Remember, I'm a judge! It's just one conviction after another around here.

STAN: I'm talking about a spiritual conviction. People need to be reminded that there are eternal consequences for their actions, and through that reminder they experience conviction.

JUDGE *(pauses):* So?

STAN: Sooo, conviction will hopefully lead them to repentance and a change of heart.

JUDGE: I have had enough talk about your kind of conviction *and* about you threatening people with the bad place! Pastor, people come to church to get their ears tickled not to get their fannies fried.

STAN: I'm not threatening people, I'm warning them.

JUDGE: Well, let me give you a warning right now. Keep your mouth shut.

STAN: If I kept my mouth shut, it would have a disastrous effect on my ministry.

JUDGE: Yeah, but maybe you'd be able to end on time for a change. Which brings me to your other charge. *(Holding papers)* It says here that you have gone 10 minutes past your allotted preaching time for the last two Sundays in a row. Are we starting a new trend here?

STAN: No, not a trend, really. I just preach as long as the Spirit leads me to.

JUDGE: Well, your Spirit needs to learn shorthand then, because for 20-odd years the Spirit in this church has both come and been gone before noon.

STAN: Change is good for the soul.

JUDGE: I thought conviction was good for the soul? Make up yer mind. Ya can't have them both . . . in fact, ya can't have neither. Change is good in my pocket and convictions are good in my prison, but I don't want either of them in my church! Now, do you have anything sensible at all to say in your defense?

STAN: No, I don't have anything to say in defense of myself, but I would like to go on record as saying that you can judge the heart of a church by judging the heart of its members.

JUDGE: Well, whoop-de-do and fiddledeedee, the only judge around here is me.

BAILIFF *(laughs):* That's a good one, Judge.

JUDGE: Thank you, Bobby Ray.

BAILIFF: Yeah, 'cuz it rhymed and everything.

JUDGE: Thanks.

BAILIFF: And it were funny too.

JUDGE: Bobby Ray, have you been taking talking lessons from the pastor here, or are you done?

BAILIFF: I think I'm done, Judge.

JUDGE: Are ya sure?

BAILIFF *(pauses long while thinking):* Yeah, I'm sure.

JUDGE: Good, then I'll proceed with the sentencing.

STAN: Well, it's about time.

JUDGE *(sarcastic):* Oh, has this been taking too long for you, Pastor? Just pretend you're in church. *(Slams gavel)* I rule guilty on both charges, of having a potty-mouth *and* having a runny one. I hereby sentence you to two weeks at the Greater Monks Monastery where you will take a temporary vow of silence.

STAN *(shocked):* A vow of silence?

JUDGE: Yeah! Hopefully you'll learn that if ya can't say something nice to your congregation, you're better off to not say nuttin' at all. And who knows, maybe you'll even learn how to tell time while you're there. Bailiff, take this man and shave an itty-bitty bald spot on the top of his head and give him to the monks! Court's adjourned!

(All three exit.)

GRANNY GLOCKENSPIEL NO. 2
A Very Good Book

Characters:

11-17-02

GRANNY GLOCKENSPIEL *Pauline Jordan*
JOE *Bucky Jordan*

Setting: A peaceful rest bench in a local mall

Props: Paperback Bible

Costumes: GRANNY: Leopard-print clothing, especially jumpsuits. She also likes rhinestones, gaudy jewelry, spandex, big scarves, really big hair, red nails, and always wears white tennis shoes. Use body padding to comical effect. JOE: Contemporary clothing.

(JOE *is seated on the bench comfortably reading his book.* GRANNY *enters from back of congregation walking very energetically. She makes it to center stage and stops to do some stretches next to* JOE. *He tries to act like he doesn't notice her, which only makes her more determined to be seen. She stretches next to him and tries to see what book he's reading, but he turns his back to her.*)

GRANNY: Beautiful day. (JOE *ignores her.*) I said, it's a beautiful day.

JOE *(looks up):* It's raining. *(Goes back to book)*

GRANNY: Inside the mall, I mean.

JOE *(looks up):* Oh. *(Back to book)*

GRANNY: I've been walking all morning.

JOE: Mmm-hmm.

GRANNY: Inside the mall. *(A beat)* Where it isn't raining. *(Pause)* Walked all the way down to Sears and back three times. (JOE *keeps ignoring her.*) Mind if I sit down? (JOE *looks at her, then scoots over to give her room.*) Thanks. *(A beat)* I've been walking all morning. *(Pause)* All the way down to Sears and back *(a beat)* three times.

JOE *(looking up, slightly annoyed):* I heard you the first time, you know.

GRANNY: You heard me the first time, what?

JOE: I heard you the first time when you said you walked to Sears. (*Goes back to book*)

GRANNY: Oh, excuse me. (*A beat*) I didn't mean to repeat myself. (JOE *scoots a little away.*) Because repeating myself isn't something I normally do. (JOE *still ignores her. She speaks louder.*) Because repeating myself isn't something I normally do!

JOE: I heard you!

GRANNY: Oh. (*A beat*) Good. (*Long pause*) Because it's just a stereotype, you know.

JOE: What is?

GRANNY: That old people sit around repeating themselves.

JOE: Oh. (*Back to book*)

GRANNY: That's just a stereotype. (*Long pause*) Of course they probably don't call it a stereotype now, though. (*A beat*) Nobody uses records anymore. (*A beat*) Not since they invented CDs. (*A beat*) So I guess it's a "CDtype." (JOE *looks at her and rolls his eyes, but she doesn't notice because she is now rubbing her feet.* JOE *goes back to book.* GRANNY *pauses.*) I've been walking all morning. (*Pause*) All the way to Sears and back . . .

JOE (*interrupting, irritated*): . . . Three times! I know!

GRANNY (*surprised*): Were you following me?

JOE (*looking at her*): No. You told me.

GRANNY: Why on earth would I bother a stranger with that?

JOE (*back to book*): I don't know.

big pause

GRANNY (*pause*): Whatcha reading?

JOE (*not looking at her*): A book.

GRANNY: Oh. (*Pause*) Is it any good?

JOE (*looking up*): What?

GRANNY: The book? Is it any good?

JOE (*irritated*): It's fine. Look Mrs. . . . Mrs. . . .

GRANNY: Glockenspiel. Mrs. Glockenspiel. But people just call me Granny.

JOE: OK, look, Granny . . .

GRANNY: And what's your name?

JOE: Joe.

GRANNY: Joe, huh?

JOE: Yes, my name is Joe.

GRANNY: Can I call ya Bob?

JOE: But I just said my name was Joe.

GRANNY: I heard you! It's just easier for me if I can call everyone Bob.

JOE: Was your husband's name Bob?

GRANNY: No, it was Frank. (JOE *goes back to book.*)

JOE: Oh.

GRANNY: But I called him Bob.

(JOE *just looks at her and slowly turns his head back to his book.*)

GRANNY: Soooooo . . . (JOE *looks up*) let me ask you somethinnnnngggg . . .(*trying to remember his name*) . . . umm . . . umm.

JOE (*finishes for her*): Bob.

GRANNY (*remembering*): Bob. Yes, Bob, let me ask ya something, Bob.

JOE: Go ahead.

GRANNY: Is the book any good?

JOE: Yes, it's a good book.

GRANNY (*pause*): How good?

JOE: Very, very good. (*Goes back to reading*)

GRANNY (*pause*): But on a scale of 1 to 10?

JOE (*angry*): It's a 10! This book is a total 10, OK!

GRANNY: OK! (*Pauses while* JOE *goes back to reading*) Ten means good, then?

JOE: Yes! Ten means good! In fact, this book is so very, very good that I would like nothing more on this earth than to be reading it! But I can't! I can't! Do you hear me? It is impossible for me to read this book! (*He glares at* GRANNY, *who looks shocked by his outburst. He catches himself and takes a deep breath before apologizing.*) I'm sorry.

GRANNY: You shouldn't be sorry. (*Patting his back*) It's not your fault the school system failed ya.

JOE: What?

GRANNY: My husband couldn't read either.

JOE: What are you talking about?

GRANNY: But at least it makes sense now.

JOE: What makes sense?

GRANNY: Well, I was wondering why you never turned the page, and if ya can't read, it makes sense.

JOE: Look, Lady! I can read! I can read!

GRANNY: Praise the Lord, you've been healed!

JOE: No! I could always read! I love to read! I would love to be reading right now, but I can't because I keep getting interrupted by you! *(Goes back to reading his book)*

GRANNY: Well, excuse me! *(They exchange glares. He goes back to book. She waits a beat.)* I didn't mean to interrupt ya. *(Pause)* 'Cause you're so busy. *(Pause)* Reading your book. *(Pause)* You're very, very, very good book that I was just asking the title of. *(Pause)* I like books, too, you know. *(Pause)* 'Cuz I like to read. *(A beat)* Books, that is. I like to read books. *(He glares up at her again.)* Especially good books.

JOE *(has finally had it and explodes):* Then here! Take mine! Take my book! You can have it! Read my book, please! Now, my very, very, very good book is yours!

GRANNY: Thank you, Bob.

JOE: Joe!

GRANNY *(correcting him):* No, Granny. Do I look like a Joe?

JOE *(stands up):* That's it! I've had it! Good-bye! (JOE *exits angrily.*)

GRANNY *(sweetly):* Good-bye, Bob. Thanks for the book. *(Looking at book)* That was very Christian of him to give me his book. *(Sighs)* Let's see what this book is . . . *(She stands up and gets her glasses out, then extends book as far away from her as possible and reads the title.)* Holly . . . Bibble . . . *(trying to read them together)*. No, that's not right . . . *(Reading again)* Holy . . . *(a beat)* . . . Bible . . . *(Making the connection)* Oh! Holy Bible? Well, that's a surprise. In paperback even. *(A beat)* Let's see what it says. *(She's starting to walk off-stage slowly while reading out loud.)* "So put on a heart of compassion, kindness, humility, gentleness and patience." *(She stops in her tracks and looks up at audience.)* That guy really should have read this. *(A beat)* He could have used it.

(She exits walking energetically through congregation.)

JUDGE MENTAL NO. 4
The Problem with Prayer

Characters:
> JUDGE MENTAL
> STAN MORRISON: *pastor*
> BAILIFF (BOBBY RAY)

Setting: Courtroom

Props: Gavel

Costumes: JUDGE wears a black robe (graduation gown). BAILIFF wears tan pants and shirt with a badge. STAN is dressed in contemporary clothing.

(BAILIFF *enters and stands at attention with hands behind him.*)

BAILIFF *(to congregation):* All rise! *(If they don't rise, BAILIFF will persist until they do!)* The Court of Popular Opinion is now in session. The Honorable Judge Mental is now presiding. (BAILIFF *stands still;* JUDGE *enters.*)

JUDGE *(sits and shuffles through papers on desk; looks at congregation and then hits gavel):* You may be seated. Docket No. 56, *The Church v. Pastor Stan Morrison.* Is the defendant present?

STAN *(seated in the congregation, he rises):* Yes, your Honor.

JUDGE: The defendant will please approach the bench and be seated. *(He does so.)* Pastor, I'm sure you're wondering what you are doing here in my court again. *(Shuffling through papers on desk)* And right now I'm wondering the same thing. Bobby Ray, have you been in my desk again?

BAILIFF: No, Judge, I sure ain't.

JUDGE: Well, then where are on earth are my papers?

BAILIFF: They're underneath the comic section.

JUDGE *(looks and finds them):* Thank you, Bobby Ray. *(Pauses)* Hey, if you weren't in my desk, how did you know they was underneath the comic section?

BAILIFF: 'Cuz that's where I left them when I wasn't there.

JUDGE: Oh. Very good. Now, let's see here . . . *(reading)* Oh my! Oh my, my, my, my, my. Well, this time the charges against you appear to be very serious. Excessive use of force is what I got here.

STAN: What on earth are you talking about?

JUDGE: Oh, trying to plead ignorance, huh? That's not going to work here. You happen to be talking to someone who has dealt with ignorance for years.

STAN: Personal experience does tend to make one an authority.

JUDGE *(proudly and not understanding the insult):* Oh, well, thank you.

STAN: My pleasure.

JUDGE *(gentlemanly):* To be sure. Now, back to these charges of excessive use of force. It appears that last Sunday at the end of service you exerted your authority as a pastor and insisted that everyone repeat a prayer after you, is that right?

STAN: Well, yes, I did, but I wouldn't really call it . . .

JUDGE: A simple yes or no will do. Now, Pastor, about this prayer you forced everyone to repeat . . . I was just wondering if'n you was aware that it was the sinner's prayer you was praying?

STAN: Yes, is there something wrong with having people repeating the sinner's prayer?

JUDGE: Oh, I suppose not . . . if the person repeating it is a *sinner,* and I ain't.

STAN: You are too.

JUDGE: Ain't neither.

STAN: Are too.

JUDGE: I said I ain't!

STAN: You are a sinner, we all are, and none of us is without sin. Now, the main reason I had the whole congregation say the sinner's prayer together was so that none of the people who were accepting Christ for the first time would feel awkward or isolated about it.

JUDGE: There ain't nothing wrong with feeling awkward and isolated. Bobby Ray feels that way all the time. Don't ya, Bobby Ray?

BAILIFF: Umm . . . uh . . . umm . . .

JUDGE: See? He's awkward and he's got but one thought in his entire head, so he's isolated too. So what?

STAN: Well, anyway, what I was trying to say is that if you think about it, you were actually helping new believers by praying with them like that.

JUDGE: I was helping?

STAN: Yes.

JUDGE: Why should I care about helping some dirty old sinner?

STAN: I suppose it would be out of the goodness of your heart, or maybe to earn some more jewels for your crown in heaven.

JUDGE: Jewels?

BAILIFF: Jewels?

STAN: Jewels.

JUDGE: That's a hoss of a different color! Did ya here that, Bailiff? Jewels!

BAILIFF: I want me some.

JUDGE: Shut your greedy old yap. Well, I'm gonna earn me another one of them jewels and let you go then, 'cuz you obviously didn't do nothing wrong . . . this time.

STAN: Thank you.

JUDGE: But, uh, Pastor, for future reference, next time ya do something like this, I'd appreciate if you'd run it by me first, that way we could avoid any misuse of valuable court time. Case dismissed! (STAN *exits.*) Hey, Bobby Ray, did ya see that? I just got me some more of them jewels!

BAILIFF *(depressed):* Yep, that sure is nice.

JUDGE: Now what's the matter with you.

BAILIFF: Well, you got yourself a whole bunch of them jewels, and I didn't get me any.

JUDGE: Hmm . . . how about I sell ya some?

BAILIFF: OK.

JUDGE: Gimme 50 bucks.

(BAILIFF *gives it to him.*)

JUDGE: There, ya happy?

BAILIFF: Where's my jewels?

JUDGE: They're in heaven, stupid.

BAILIFF: Do I have as many as you now?

JUDGE: Nope, I got me a few more right now just for being nice and selling 'em to ya.

BAILIFF: That ain't fair.

JUDGE: Well, ya can always buy more and try to catch up.

BAILIFF: I'll go git my wallet.

JUDGE *(shakes his head and says to himself about BAILIFF):* It's like watching my favorite cartoon.

(*They exit.*)

SERGEANT SALVATION
Episode Three: Off to the Races

Characters:
SARGE
TOM
HEATHER

Setting: After hours at church

Props: A pew or bench, Kentucky Fried Chicken bucket, checkbook, wallet, pen, play money, 2 tithe envelopes, whistle

SARGE *(yells while entering at a rapid pace, thinking his "troupe" is following behind him):* Aaaaaaaaaaaaaaattention! I want all new baby Christians in formation and toeing the line! *Now!* Move, move, move, and move! *(Stops center stage to face the audience)* Welcome to Basic Christianity Boot Camp. My name is Sergeant Salvation, and for the next few weeks I'll be your authority figure, your mentor, your drill instructor, and for some of you, I'll be your worst nightmare. *(He spins around quickly and notices he's alone. He marches offstage immediately and comes back pushing the new recruits out before him.)* Move, move, move, move, move!

TOM: It's not my fault! *(Pointing to HEATHER)* I was trying to get her.

SARGE *(looks at HEATHER):* Private Heather! Do you have an explanation for your failure to follow a direct command?

HEATHER: Well, you were the one who said "about-face." I just assumed that meant to check my makeup.

SARGE: Hush up, both of ya! You're wasting my time, and the material we are covering this week is crucial, so let's get started. Now, we're gonna use this here to represent the offering bucket. *(Holding up a Kentucky Fried Chicken bucket)* Which of you biblical scholar wannabes knows how this works?

HEATHER: I do! That's where we get to put in our tithes and offering for the furthering of God's kingdom, right?

SARGE: No, that is not right! I didn't ask why we do it, I asked how we do it! Listen up, Private! Now, there are certain rules to the passing of the offering. Rule No. 1: You must have checks prepared *before* coming to church so's ya don't slow down the passing of the plate. Rule No. 2: Ya gotta be quick about filling out the tithe envelope so's ya don't slow down the passing of the plate! Rule No. 3: Ya don't slow down the passing of the plate! *(Holds up tithe envelope)* Now, who knows what this is?

TOM: A letter to your mother?

SARGE: No, maggots! This here is the tithe envelope! If ya don't want people to know what you're giving to God, then ya put it in here! I personally like everyone to know what I'm putting in so I can get some extraspecial respect! Now we are gonna run some timed relays on filling out and putting in these envelopes . . . and do you know why?

BOTH: So's we don't slow down the passing of the plate!

SARGE: Exactly right! Now here are your envelopes . . . you have five seconds to get your tithe out, put it in the envelope, place it in the offering, and pass the bucket on! Ready?

BOTH: Ready!

SARGE *(blows whistle):* Go!

(HEATHER and TOM hurriedly attempt to complete the task. This is a mocking of the putting a rifle together drill in the army. SARGE begins to count off.)

SARGE: One saint going to heaven, two sinners going to hell, three saints going to heaven, four sinners going to hell, five saints going to heaven! *(Blows whistle)* Time!

HEATHER *(jumps up excitedly):* Wahoo! Done! Yay! I did it!

(TOM is still writing his check out.)

SARGE: What are you doing, Boy?

TOM: Um, I'm still writing my check out.

SARGE: No! You are to do that before you get to church! Now, I want you to drop and give me a hundred!

(TOM drops to floor.)

TOM: A hundred what?

SARGE: A hundred cash! I want you to give till it hurts!

(TOM drops to floor and gets wallet out and hands it up to him.)

TOM *(gives him another hundred):* Uh, I'm sure hurting now, Sarge.

SARGE: Good! Now get up!

HEATHER *(stands up):* Pardon me, Sarge, but I was just thinking . . .

SARGE *(interrupting):* Pardon me, Missy, but who asked you to think?

HEATHER: This will only take a second.

SARGE: Very well, proceed.

HEATHER: OK, what I was . . .

SARGE *(looks at watch and cuts her off):* Time! Now, one thing that I find completely unacceptable is when some annoying little Christian drops change instead of bills into the bucket. The plinking noise that accompanies the sound of silver hitting tin is distracting to the entire congregation. Plinking sounds should be completely avoided unless it's a plinking sound of the car keys to a brand-new Mercedes being dropped in the bucket. And mind you, that don't happen nearly often enough.

TOM: My uncle has a used Buick sitting in his backyard that he wants to get rid of.

SARGE: I'll bet he has a nephew sitting in his front yard he wants to get rid of too. Regardless, neither would be appropriate for the bucket.

HEATHER: Is it all right if I say something now?

SARGE: Are you still thinking? All right then, go ahead before your little brain explodes.

HEATHER: Thank you.

SARGE *(interrupting):* Far be it from me to keep someone from speaking his or her mind.

HEATHER: I appreciate that.

SARGE *(interrupting):* I'm a modern man and appreciate what a woman has to say.

HEATHER: Very understanding of you . . .

SARGE *(interrupting):* I get complimented on it all the time.

HEATHER: OK, we get it! You're an incredible human being! Now can I speak?

SARGE: Permission granted.

HEATHER: I was thinking that I don't mind giving my tithes and offerings to God at all. It's an honor actually, but it's my personal opinion that it should be done out of a thankful heart and not by bullying it out of us.

SARGE *(pauses):* Permission withdrawn. Disregard my thoughtfulness on speaking your mind while we all disregard you.

TOM: I don't know, Sarge, I think she's right.

SARGE: Now you're thinking too? Just a couple of little thinkers, aren't ya? Nothing better to do than sit around and think on my time! This is becoming a little mental mutiny on the brainy, isn't it?

HEATHER: I'm just saying . . .

SARGE (*interrupts by placing bucket back over* HEATHER's *head and cutting her off*): Now, Tom, I hope you aren't planning on questioning my authority, too, because there ain't room enough under this bucket for the both of ya.

TOM (*not registering at first*): Huh?

SARGE (*mimicking* TOM): Huh? What kinda answer is huh? I asked you a direct question, Private! You either answer yes Sir or no Sir, but if you absolutely have to say huh, then you will say huh Sir! Got it?

TOM (*shocked*): Uh-huh. (SARGE *glares at him.*) I mean, yes Sir, I've got it! And no Sir, I do not wish to join Heather under the bucket! I am not questioning your authority, Sir!

HEATHER (*to* TOM *while removing the bucket from her head*): Traitor!

SARGE: Let's get something straight, Missy. I don't care what's in your heart. And I don't care what's in Tom's wallet. All I care about is what goes in this here bucket, and it better not go plink! There is nothing more frustrating than dealing with a couple of skin-flinted, penny-pinching, miserminded Christians. (HEATHER *throws the bucket on the floor in frustration.*) Hey! Careful with that, it cost me a quarter!

TOM (*changing the subject*): Sarge, how do you know how much money to put in the bucket?

SARGE: Well, the Bible says 10 percent, so 10 percent it is.

HEATHER: What about an offering?

SARGE: That depends, whatcha offering?

HEATHER: No, not me, all of us . . . an offering unto the Lord.

SARGE: I hate to quote Tom, but . . . huh?

HEATHER: An offering is an amount given out of love *beyond* the normal tithe.

SARGE: You don't think I know that? Of course I know that! That's exactly why I always round my tithe up to the nearest penny. That way ya kill two birds with one check made payable to the church but not cashable till Friday.

HEATHER: The offering is also a way of . . .

SARGE: Are we supposed to sit here and listen to you spewing thoughts on this subject until you are completely satisfied that your voice has been heard?

HEATHER: That would be nice, yes.

SARGE (*looks at watch*): Oh, look, time to go.

TOM: But we've only been in class for five minutes.

HEATHER (to TOM): He's about as generous with his time as he is with his money.

TOM: Actually, it was my money he was being generous with.

SARGE: No need to thank me, I'm just doing my duty. Class dismissed.

TOM: Umm . . . Sarge, about my money . . .

SARGE: Are you so petty that you require a receipt for your tax records?

TOM: Yes, I guess I am.

SARGE (checking pockets): Fine, then. Heather, give him one. I don't have any paper.

HEATHER: I don't have any paper either.

TOM: What about using this bus schedule I found on the floor?

HEATHER: Hey! (Takes the piece of paper) This isn't a bus schedule, it's a schedule for the horse races.

SARGE: Oops, gimme that, it's mine.

HEATHER: What's a Christian doing at the racetrack?

SARGE: Witnessing! And Tom's generous offering is making that possible. Aaaaaaaatttteeeennnttttion! Left face! Forward march! (They exit.)

JUDGE MENTAL NO. 5
A Rude Awakening

Characters:
> JUDGE MENTAL
> MILLIE MULLIGAN
> BAILIFF (BOBBY RAY)

Setting: Courtroom

Props: Gavel

Costumes: JUDGE wears a black robe (graduation gown). BAILIFF wears tan pants and shirt with a badge. MILLIE is dressed in contemporary clothing.

(BAILIFF *enters and stands at attention with hands behind him.*)

BAILIFF *(to congregation):* All rise! *(If they don't rise,* BAILIFF *will persist until they do!)* The Court of Popular Opinion is now in session. The Honorable Judge Mental is now presiding. (BAILIFF *stands still;* JUDGE *enters.*)

JUDGE *(sits and shuffles through papers on desk; looks at congregation and then hits gavel):* You may be seated. Docket No. 57, *The Church v. Millie Mulligan.* Is that no-good lowlife in the courtroom?

MILLIE *(seated in the congregation, she rises):* Uh . . . yes. Yes, your Honor.

JUDGE: The defendant will please approach the bench and be seated. *(She does so.)* Now, Miss Mulligan, you have been charged with committing a heinous crime. Bailiff, tell her what that means.

BAILIFF *(singsongy):* You're in trouble; you're in trouble!

MILLIE: There must be some misunderstanding . . .

JUDGE: Hush up! Bobby Ray, let's play a game. I'm gonna tell you a story about this here lady and let's see if you can figure out what the charges are that I brought against her.

BAILIFF: I like games.

JUDGE: Last Sunday morning I was in church resting comfortably in my favorite pew when Pastor Morrison began to preach.

BAILIFF: What was the pastor preaching about?

JUDGE: Don't know; don't matter. All I know is I was serene and tranquil and I soon found myself all snuggled up in my pew sound asleep dreaming about my mama's fritters.

BAILIFF: They sure are good.

JUDGE: Yep, sure are. Now, Pastor was *halfway through* his sermon when suddenly this woman here comes along and wakes me up! Now, Bobby Ray, have you figured out what the charges against this lady are?

BAILIFF: Yup, this lady here is guilty of neglect.

JUDGE: What? Where on earth did you get that?

BAILIFF: She shouldn't have let you sleep through half of Pastor's sermon, she should have woken you up a lot sooner. She's guilty of neglect!

JUDGE: Neglect? Bobby Ray, that is *so* not the point of my story.

BAILIFF: It isn't?

JUDGE: No, she shouldn't have woken me up sooner; the point is that she shouldn't have woken me up at all!

BAILIFF: Oh.

JUDGE: This woman here isn't guilty of neglect!

BAILIFF: She isn't?

JUDGE: No! She's being charged with disturbing my peace!

BAILIFF: That's miiiiighty serious.

JUDGE: You bet it is!

BAILIFF (*to* MILLIE): Ya ought not to have done that, Ma'am.

MILLIE: I had to! His snoring was disrupting the entire service!

JUDGE: Liar! I do not snore! Never have! You have just now added perjury to your charges.

MILLIE: Perjury?

JUDGE: Perjury! You do know what that is, don't ya? Bobby Ray, explain it to her.

BAILIFF: Well, umm . . . it's uh . . . it's umm . . . bad.

JUDGE: Thank you for that excellent explanation, Bobby Ray, but how about next time you be less wordy?

BAILIFF: Sorry, Judge.

JUDGE (*to* MILLIE): Then that makes two of ya who's sorry, because you, Ma'am, are a sorry, sad, pathetic, twisted individual who just can't stand to see a fellow human being resting comfortably. Therefore I must punish you with a sentence befitting the crime.

MILLIE: Now, wait just a minute . . .

JUDGE: Wait just a minute? I don't have a minute. My time is valuable.

MILLIE: What about my time?

JUDGE: The only time you need to be worried about is your time in jail and how you're gonna go about serving it.

MILLIE: Jail? (*To* BAILIFF) Did he just say "jail"?

JUDGE: What are ya asking him for? I said it!

MILLIE: There must be some mistake.

JUDGE: Oh, there was a mistake, all right, and you're the one who made it. I hereby rule that this lady is guilty of disturbing my peace and order her to serve out 10 days in the county jail where she will most certainly not be resting comfortably.

MILLIE (*unbelieving*): Ten days?

JUDGE: Twenty days?

MILLIE (*unbelieving*): Twenty days?

JUDGE: OK, 30 days, but that's my final offer. (*Slams gavel*) Sold! Oh, and Miss Mulligan?

MILLIE (*depressed*): Yes, Sir?

JUDGE: I will also be assigning a guard to your cell whose only duty will be to wake you up every hour on the hour in order to disturb your peace. Now we'll just see how much you like it! (*Slams gavel*) Court's adjourned. Bailiff, take this woman into custody and make sure she gets some of those nice striped pajamas. I'm gonna go take me a little nap.

(*All exit.*)

GRANNY GLOCKENSPIEL NO. 3

Yakkety-Yak

Characters:
GRANNY GLOCKENSPIEL
SANDY

Setting: A peaceful rest bench in a local mall

Props: Exercise bag, 2 pair of cheap white canvas tennis shoes

Costumes: GRANNY: Leopard-print clothes, especially jumpsuits or a sweat suit with rhinestones, gaudy jewelry, spandex, big scarves, really big hair, red nails, and always wears white tennis shoes. Use body padding to comical effect. SANDY: Contemporary clothing.

(GRANNY *walks in energetically through the congregation. She takes a seat on her bench center stage and rummages through her exercise bag.*)

GRANNY: That's it. Got my exercise in for today, but I am a little disappointed that I didn't get to talk to anyone. *(Yells up at God)* Hey! I'm getting ready to leave now! It's Your last chance! *(Pause)* Must be busy. *(Shrugs)* Oh well. At least I can get out of these shoes. They're killing me. *(She takes off both of her white tennis shoes and sets them on the bench beside her. While her back is turned* SANDY *comes and sits beside her.* GRANNY *doesn't notice and reaches in the bag and pulls out a new pair of tennis shoes that are completely identical to the others and she puts them on.)* There! That's better! (SANDY *hands her the other pair to put in her bag.* GRANNY *doesn't realize that someone is handing them to her.)* Thank you.

SANDY: You're welcome.

GRANNY *(looking in bag at shoes)*: God? *(Pause)* Your voice is a little higher than I thought it would be.

SANDY *(tapping* GRANNY *on shoulder)*: Over here.

GRANNY *(notices* SANDY *for the first time)*: Ssshhhh! I'm talking to God. *(Talking back into bag)* Are ya still there? Hello? Helloooooo? Hmm . . . He must have gotten busy again. *(She zips exercise bag up.)*

SANDY: Are you . . . *(looking at business card)* Granny Glockenspiel, Mall Missionary?

GRANNY: Yep, that's me. Hey, you got one of my cards!

SANDY: Yes, I was referred.

GRANNY: Well, good, what can I help you with?

SANDY: Well, it's my friend. She and I got in a little argument a few days ago, so I came to you for advice.

GRANNY: Well, I'm very flattered that you . . .

SANDY (interrupting): I just want to go on record as saying that I forgive her although she hasn't exactly asked for my forgiveness yet.

GRANNY: I'm sure she . . .

SANDY (interrupting): See, she called this special lunch where we were supposed to meet because she said she had something serious to discuss.

GRANNY: And what exactly . . . ?

SANDY (interrupting): Did we have for lunch? Well, we were at a Chinese restaurant and she had the tuna sushi and I had a small salad.

GRANNY: Is that the . . . ?

SANDY (interrupting): Standard fare for both of us? Yes, I'm a vegetarian, but she's only a partial one and thus the fish she ordered.

GRANNY: I meant, what was the . . . ?

SANDY (interrupting): Total cost? I'm not sure, we went dutch.

GRANNY: You went dutch to a Chinese place?

SANDY: Yes.

GRANNY: Did ya have to remove your clogs?

SANDY: What?

GRANNY: Just trying to derail your thoughts for a minute. Now, let's cut to the chase, Sweetie. What was the fight about?

SANDY: Well! She sat there, right across from me, in the middle of this restaurant, with her tuna sushi getting warm and she looked me right in the eyes . . .

GRANNY: What was it about?

SANDY: It was about talking.

GRANNY: Talking?

SANDY: Or listening. I'm not quite sure which. I think both.

GRANNY: I see.

SANDY: She said something to the effect that I talked too much and listened too little—which really upset me—so for the next five minutes I told her exactly how I felt about that and then stormed off before she could say a word.

GRANNY: I guess you were determined to prove her point.

SANDY: Exactly, and now our friendship is broken beyond repair. Do you have any solutions at all?

GRANNY: Yes, duct tape.

SANDY: I was speaking figuratively about the friendship being broken.

GRANNY: It's not for the friendship, it's for that pretty little mouth of yours. Mere lipstick doesn't do it justice.

SANDY: Duct tape? For my mouth? *(Pause)* That was a very rude thing to say. In fact, that could very possibly be one of the rudest things anyone has ever said to me. Although there was that one time when I was standing in the express lane at the grocery store with 8 items or less and there was this one person who had 16 items and crowded in front of me. I told them that 8 items was the limit for the express lane, and they told me to mind my own business. I thought that was very rude too. (GRANNY *gets up and starts circling the bench while* SANDY *is seated.* GRANNY *is looking for something.)* But you definitely take the cake on rudeness. (GRANNY *pushes* SANDY *forward on the bench and looks behind* SANDY.) Speaking of rude, it's *very* rude to be up and moving around and not focusing on a person when the person is trying to speak with you about how rude you are. (GRANNY *gets on the floor and looks under the bench.)* How would you like it if you were the one who was upset and then someone said something rude to you? (SANDY *is exasperated.)* What *are* you looking for?

GRANNY: Your off switch or a plug, either one will do.

SANDY: That's it. You have offended me for the last time. I'm leaving. *(Starts to get up)*

GRANNY *(pushes* SANDY *back down on bench):* Oh no you're not, sister. You're gonna sit right there and let me get a word in edgewise.

SANDY: How dare you . . . ?

GRANNY *(interrupting):* . . . Talk to you like that? It's a wonder anyone talks to you at all, with the self-centered attitude you have.

SANDY: Well, I never . . .

GRANNY *(interrupting):* . . . Had anyone say that to you before? I find that hard to believe.

SANDY: This is the final . . .

GRANNY *(interrupting):* . . . Word on the matter? I'll bet that's a phrase you don't use much.

SANDY: You'd better . . .

GRANNY *(interrupting):* . . . Tell it like it is? Oh, I do, don't you worry about that. Now, you find this friend of yours and you apologize for your selfish behavior. Got it? Then take some time to learn how to listen to someone else for a change. You might just learn something for yourself.

SANDY *(pauses while looking at her):* Wow.

GRANNY: Wow?

SANDY: Wow, no one has ever talked to me like that before.

GRANNY: Oh, I'm sure they have. You just didn't stick around to hear it.

SANDY: I don't even know how to apologize. I've never done it before. How do I do it?

GRANNY: Well, why don't you try asking God?

SANDY: Ask God? Does He answer?

GRANNY: Only if you're listening.

SANDY: OK, you're right. *(She takes* GRANNY's *exercise bag and speaks into it.)* Hello, God? It's me, Sandy, and I was wondering if You could help me. See, I was having a disagreement with a friend who isn't a friend anymore, but I want her to be a friend again, so we can be friends like friends are. *(Pause)* And, God, if You don't mind my saying so, Your breath smells really bad.

GRANNY: That's my shoes.

SANDY: Oops, never mind, Granny says it's her shoes.

GRANNY *(taking her by elbow):* Come on, I'll walk you out.

SANDY *(getting up and still talking in the exercise bag):* So, anyway, we were at lunch and she told me that I had a problem with listening too little and talking too much and after talking with Granny here I think my friend was right. What should I do? *(Pauses, then looks at* GRANNY*)* He isn't saying anything.

GRANNY: Keep listening.

SANDY: But there isn't . . .

GRANNY *(interrupting):* Just listen and don't say another word until He answers.

SANDY: Does that usually take very long?

GRANNY: Only till I reach my car, Sweetie, only till I reach my car.

JUDGE MENTAL NO. 6
Solitary Confinement

Characters:
 JUDGE MENTAL
 REGGIE GRAGABOLWITZ
 BAILIFF (BOBBY RAY)

Setting: Courtroom

Props: Gavel

Costumes: JUDGE wears a black robe (graduation gown). BAILIFF wears tan pants and shirt with a badge. REGGIE is dressed in contemporary clothing.

(BAILIFF enters and stands at attention with hands behind him.)

BAILIFF *(to congregation):* All rise! *(If they don't rise, BAILIFF will persist until they do!)* The Court of Popular Opinion is now in session. The Honorable Judge Mental is now presiding. *(BAILIFF stands still; JUDGE enters.)*

JUDGE *(sits and shuffles through papers on desk; looks at congregation and then hits gavel):* You may be seated. Docket No. 58, *The Church v. Reggie* G . . . G . . . *(Problems pronouncing last name) Gagarble . . . Gragable . . . Gribuble . . . (Gives up) The Church v. Reggie.* Is the defendant present?

REGGIE *(seated in the congregation, he rises):* Right here, your Honor.

JUDGE: The defendant will please approach the bench and be seated. (REGGIE *does so.)* I understand that you've been charged with the repeated offense of nuptial ducking. Is that true?

REGGIE: Nuptial ducking?

JUDGE: Nuptial ducking! Says here that you are 31 years of age and yet you remain unbetrothed!

BAILIFF: Now there's a sticky sityation!

REGGIE: Not really.

JUDGE: Are you against marriage, Son?

REGGIE: Not at all, Sir.

JUDGE: Good, cause it's a wonderful way to be institutionalized. I mean it's a wonderful institution. How have you come to avoid it?

REGGIE: I just haven't met the right woman.

JUDGE: If we all sat around waiting for the right woman, ain't none of us would be married. Isn't that right, Bobby Ray?

BAILIFF: That sure enough is.

JUDGE: What type of wife are you looking for?

REGGIE: Well, first of all, I'm not looking right now . . .

JUDGE: And why not? You think they're gonna come looking for you? Is your last name Trump?

REGGIE: No.

JUDGE: Gates?

REGGIE: No.

JUDGE: How about Kennedy?

REGGIE: My last name is Gragabolwitz.

JUDGE *(pause):* I'd start looking. *(Pause)* Now, what type of woman appeals to ya?

REGGIE: I don't know. I haven't really thought about it much, but I suppose it would be for a woman who places Jesus first in her life and is concerned with the needs of others.

JUDGE: Sir, I think your problem is that you're unwilling to settle. I settled. At first I was determined to hold out for a Sophia Loren type, you know, beautiful and mysterious, but a few days later I met Myra, fine figure of a woman, sturdy too, can move a refrigerator by herself and don't mind answering to "Hey you." We're happy! She got the man she always dreamed of, and I . . . I settled. But you, you're 31 and still single. All the good girls are gone now. Why, at this point the only requirement you should have for a woman is that she's breathing.

REGGIE: Well, I'll be sure to keep that in mind, but for now I am completely satisfied in pursuing my credentials as a pastor and eventually leading to a position on the mission field.

JUDGE: You can't be a minister and be spouseless. It's unseemly, not to mention it would make everybody in your congregation miserable.

REGGIE: How could my remaining single make everyone else miserable?

JUDGE: Are you daft? A single man in church makes all the women miserable, which in turn makes all the men miserable, leading of course to the misery of the church's children. Now, we all know God don't want His children miserable, so that means you have to get married, hitched, saddled up, and tied down.

REGGIE: But I don't want to be married. The apostle Paul himself said it was *better* for a man *never* to marry . . .

JUDGE: Well, that's all fine and dandy, but the apostle Paul never attended *my* church and *I* say marriage is a requirement for proper sanctification, therefore I sentence you to one week at Pat Robertson's Singles Seminar in Virginia Beach.

REGGIE: A singles seminar?

JUDGE: That's right. You will then appear before me at the conclusion of the week and introduce me to your bride-to-be.

REGGIE: But I don't want to be married yet!

JUDGE: If, however, you are unsuccessful in this endeavor and continue to remain to be single, you will then be sentenced to solitary confinement where you will hopefully be able to increase your desire for human companionship. *(Slams gavel)* Court's adjourned. Bailiff, see that this man gets to the nearest foo-foo men's store.

BAILIFF: A foo-foo men's store?

JUDGE: Yeah, you know, Sears.

BAILIFF: Oh, OK.

JUDGE: And see that he gets some mismatched socks and a tie that clashes. We'll see if we can get that sloppy dresser sympathy syndrome started with these women first, to give him a head start. By the way, my anniversary is coming up, too, so pick me up something nice for Myra.

BAILIFF: Like what?

JUDGE: Like, how about a hand truck to help her out with that fridge. And put a bow on it. She oughta love me for that one.

(All exit.)

SERGEANT SALVATION
Episode Four:
Earning Your Keep

Characters:
SARGE
TOM
HEATHER

Setting: Church

Props: Plunger, mop, 2 manila envelopes marked "Top Secret" and filled with papers stapled together

Costumes: Sergeant outfit for SARGE and contemporary clothing for TOM and HEATHER

(TOM *and* HEATHER *enter marching from the back of the congregation with* SARGE *right behind them.*)

SARGE *(leading march):* Your left, your left, your left, right, left. Company halt! (TOM *and* HEATHER *stop.*) Fall in! (TOM *and* HEATHER *line up next to each other on the platform facing audience.*) I want all new baby Christians in formation and toeing the line! (TOM *and* HEATHER *stand at attention.*) Welcome to Basic Christianity Boot Camp. My name is Sergeant Salvation, and for the next few weeks I'll be your authority figure, your mentor, your drill instructor, and for some of you . . .

ALL *(in unison):* I'll be your worst nightmare!

SARGE *(irritated):* I see some of you have heard this before. That must make me sort of a broken record.

TOM *(laughing):* Yeah! *(Pause)* Umm . . . what's a record?

SARGE: What's a record? Oh, that's right, you call them compact discs now. Let me tell you what a record is . . . *(Yells in* TOM's *face)* The level of your stupidity! Now that's a record! You have anything to say about that?

TOM: Yeah *(wiping face)*, breath mints.

SARGE *(to* TOM): Drop to the floor!

HEATHER: Sarge, you can't make Tom give you 20 more push-ups. He's been doing them all morning.

SARGE: I didn't say anything about doing any push-ups. I just stepped on something outside and want to wipe my boots off. *(He wipes them on* TOM's *back.)* All right, Private, you can get up now.

TOM *(getting up):* Thanks. *(Sarcastic)* I'm glad I could be of service.

SARGE: Me, too, and as a matter of fact, I'm glad you mentioned that word, because that's exactly what I'm going to be talking about today . . . service.

HEATHER: You mean how we're to go about service to the Lord through our actions and abilities?

SARGE *(rolling his eyes):* It just gets so tiring dealing with the unchurched. *(Yelling)* No, that's not what I mean! I'm talking about a building of this magnitude requiring a lot of upkeep! Now, just who do you think performs that service?

HEATHER: We do?

SARGE: Exactly!

TOM: Couldn't we just hire a janitor?

SARGE: Hire a janitor? Don't you know that hiring someone costs money?

HEATHER: Well, what's wrong with that?

SARGE *(mimicking* HEATHER): "Well, what's wrong with that?" *(Yelling)* I'll tell ya what's wrong with that! If the church is spending money hiring janitors, less money is going to the mission field! If less money were going to the mission field, our very own missionaries would be starving to death. Is that what you want?

TOM: Well, no . . . of course not, but . . .

SARGE *(interrupting):* I think it is! You both wouldn't mind if some skinny missionaries of ours were sitting around at dinnertime gnawing on a piece of cardboard saying, "We could have had rice tonight, but those lazy Christians at Cozy Creek Community Church had to hire a janitor."

HEATHER: Sarge, that's ridiculous . . .

SARGE: How about we just go ahead and change the Lord's prayer to "Give us this day our daily piece of rubber to melt into soup and forgive us our churches who couldn't clean after themselves." How about we do that? Huh? Huh?

TOM: Sarge, I think you're overreacting.

SARGE *(yelling):* Is that what you want?

BOTH: Sir, no Sir!

SARGE: Do we or do we not need volunteers?

BOTH: Sir, yes Sir!

SARGE: Do we or do we not need janitors?

BOTH: Sir, yes Sir!

SARGE: Well, thanks for volunteering. Here are your tools. *(Hands* TOM *the plunger and* HEATHER *the mop)* Don't forget, this is just to get you started. After that you'll have to buy your own cleaning supplies. Now, along with your volunteer duties as janitors you will also be expected to fulfill certain responsibilities within the church structure. *(Hands them each a manila folder marked "Top Secret")* This is your weekly itinerary—a list of specific functions that will be required from each of you while attending this church. Please note where your names are.

(Both open up envelopes and pull out a bunch of papers stapled together.)

HEATHER: Look at all of these!

SARGE: You have a problem, Private?

HEATHER *(looking at her list):* Umm . . . our names are on every single one of these, Sir.

SARGE: And that's right!

TOM *(referring to papers):* Look, Sarge, I'd be happy to join the choir and help serve coffee to newcomers, but I'm not in any position to start teaching a Bible class yet or to do prison ministry . . .

HEATHER: And what about all of this stuff on the last page? *(Reading)* Wash Sarge's Jeep, clean Sarge's house, mow Sarge's lawn, and fold Sarge's laundry. You can't possibly expect me to do all this stuff.

SARGE: Of course I don't expect you to do it. Give me that. *(Takes papers from* HEATHER *and switches them with* TOM*)* I expected Tom to do it. I got your duty envelopes mixed.

TOM: OK, I can see where you might not expect the church to pay for the janitor service, but the rest of this stuff has to do only with you, so certainly you're going to be paying me for it.

SARGE: I most certainly am not! I am a member of this church, and that means I am a part of it, and if I'm a part of it, that means your services go beyond the four walls of the church and extend all the way over to my house.

HEATHER *(to* TOM*):* This is *so* not fair.

SARGE: Heather! Would you like to share what you're saying with the rest of the class?

HEATHER: Tom *is* the rest of the class, Sir.

SARGE: Humph! I'm sensing some resistance to the spiritual duties assigned each of you, am I right?

TOM: I wouldn't say "resistance," actually.

HEATHER: How about downright refusal?

SARGE: Let me ask you something, Missy. If you are not willing to do the services required of you, then just exactly how do you plan on earning your way into my good graces much less earning your way into heaven?

HEATHER: That's easy, I don't.

TOM: Yeah! If we have to earn our way into heaven, then what about grace being freely given and freely received?

HEATHER *(gestures with papers):* Not to mention all the time involved in doing this stuff.

SARGE: Well, first of all, Grace does not work here, you do. And second of all, as far as your time goes, you are to freely give it while I freely receive.

HEATHER: You know, Sarge, I may be a new baby Christian, but I know better than to think I can earn my way into heaven by my works.

TOM: That's right. It's by grace that we've been saved, and we receive it through faith, not latrine service, so I quit! *(Drops plunger)*

HEATHER: I quit too! *(Drops mop)*

SARGE *(hurt):* Quitting? You're just gonna quit on me like that? Just a couple of deserters quitting the very Sarge who loves ya?

HEATHER: Loves us? Sarge, you have never sent one ounce of love in our direction!

SARGE *(starts to cry):* I know, I've failed. *(Wiping tears)* It's how I grew up; I can't express my emotions. To do so would be to admit weakness.

HEATHER: Sarge?

SARGE *(sniffling):* And now I've gone and run my two best friends out of the church completely just because I expected them to do something out of love for me and the church. Boohoo-hoo.

TOM *(softening up immediately):* I don't mind, Sarge.

HEATHER *(seriously):* I'm surprised. *(Placing hand on* SARGE's *shoulder)* Poor Sarge, you really do have a heart, don't ya?

SARGE: Yeah, and it's a great big one that's breaking all over the place right now. *(Pause)* I should never have asked you to do that stuff.

HEATHER *(becoming decisive):* We've changed our minds.

TOM *(surprised):* We have?

HEATHER: We're not quitting, and we're going to stay and see each other through this whole thing.

SARGE: Staying? Are you still going to be the janitors?

BOTH: Yes, Sir!

SARGE *(sniffling):* And clean my house?

TOM *(giving in):* OK, we'll do that too. Out of love for God . . .

HEATHER *(interrupts):* And love for you, but not because we're trying to earn anything.

TOM: It's just the smart thing to do.

HEATHER *(picks up mop):* All right, Tom, it looks like we have some bathrooms to clean.

TOM: Don't you worry about us, Sarge. We're here for ya. Well, not exactly "here" for ya, but we'll at least be in the bathroom for ya.

HEATHER: See ya tomorrow, Sarge.

(They exit.)

SARGE: Speaking of the smart thing to do. *(Reaching in pocket)* I'm sure glad I thought to grab my glycerin tears this morning or I'd be scrubbing those toilets myself. *(Laughs)* They're nice kids, though. I'm sure glad I've earned their respect. *(Exits, wiping off his remaining "tears")*

JUDGE MENTAL NO. 7
Striking Out

Characters:
> JUDGE MENTAL
> BRUCE McGRATH
> BAILIFF (BOBBY RAY)

Setting: Courtroom

Props: Gavel

Costumes: JUDGE wears a black robe (graduation gown). BAILIFF wears tan pants and shirt with a badge. BRUCE is dressed in contemporary clothing.

(BAILIFF *enters and stands at attention with hands behind him.*)

BAILIFF *(to congregation):* All rise! *(If they don't rise, BAILIFF will persist until they do!)* The Court of Popular Opinion is now in session. The Honorable Judge Mental is now presiding. (BAILIFF *stands still;* JUDGE *enters.*)

JUDGE *(sits and shuffles through papers on desk; looks at congregation and then hits gavel):* You may be seated. Docket No. 59, *The Church v. Bruce McGrath.* Is the defendant present?

BRUCE *(seated in the congregation, he rises):* Yes, your Honor.

JUDGE: The defendant will please approach the bench and be seated. (BRUCE *does so.*) You have been charged with improper use of church funds. How do you plead?

BRUCE: Well, I guess I plead innocent since I don't know what you're talking about.

JUDGE: Oh, don't plead innocent with me, Boy. You know exactly what I'm talking about. Are you or are you not the coach of a softball team at Cozy Creek Community Church?

BRUCE: Well, yes, of course I'm the coach, you know that! But what does that have to do with this charge of improper use of church funds?

JUDGE: What does a church softball team have to do with improper use of church funds? What does peanut butter have to do with jelly? Is the church financing the softball team?

BRUCE: Yes.

JUDGE: Does the good book say to take care of widows, orphans, and softball teams?

BRUCE: Well, of course not.

JUDGE: Then by your own admission you have used church funds for a softball team and have thusly taken money away from poor widows and homeless orphans.

BRUCE: Have you ever worked for the Democratic Party, by chance?

JUDGE: How dare you make such a slanderous and utterly disrespectful accusation, you wily old Billy Martin wannabe. Perhaps you could explain to me what function a church softball team could possibly serve that would justify the use of church funding?

BRUCE: There are a lot of people out there who love sports, and our softball team is a community outreach program designed to meet them right where they are.

JUDGE: I don't care about meeting people right where they are. I wanna meet them in church!

BRUCE: Your Honor, 12 years ago I came to play softball for this church and the only requirement was that I attended services, which in turn led me to getting saved.

JUDGE: Aw, I'm getting all misty. Bobby Ray, hand me a tissue.

BAILIFF: It does seem like an important program, Judge.

JUDGE: I'll be the one who decides what's important around here!

BRUCE: I don't suppose your being angry has anything to do with the fact that you didn't get picked to be pitcher, would it?

BAILIFF: You tried out for pitcher?

BRUCE: He sure did, but the poor guy throws like a sissy.

JUDGE: A sissy? I'll show you who throws like a sissy. Watch what I can do with this softball. *(Pulls softball off desk)* Bobby Ray, stand over there. *(Points to spot across stage;* BAILIFF *walks to it.)*

BAILIFF: Is this OK?

JUDGE: No, move closer. (BAILIFF *moves closer.)* I said closer! *(Moves closer still)* Can't you hear me? I said clooooooooooser! (BAILIFF *is almost standing next to him and,* JUDGE *tosses the ball lightly and hits* BAILIFF *right in the head.)*

BAILIFF: Ow!

JUDGE: Whoops. Sorry, Bobby Ray. Now, was that a ball or a strike?

BAILIFF: I'm not sure.

JUDGE: Want me to do it again?

BAILIFF: It was a strike, Judge!

JUDGE: That's right. Now, because of that eloquent speech on the importance of softball in a church you gave, Mr. McGrath, I have become convinced that it is indeed a necessary outreach program to the community.

BRUCE: Thank you, Judge . . .

JUDGE: However, because of your disrespectful and uncharitable disposition, I hereby fire you, Bruce McGrath, from your position as softball coach.

BRUCE: Fired?

JUDGE: That's right, and instead you will be replaced with Bobby Ray.

BAILIFF: I get to be coach?

JUDGE: It's to make up for the hitting ya in the head thing. That's my ruling, now court's adjourned. *(Gavel slams)* You can leave your uniform in Bobby Ray's locker on your way out. (BRUCE *exits.)*

BAILIFF: I can't believe I'm a softball coach!

JUDGE: It's exciting, isn't it?

BAILIFF: I'll say!

JUDGE: It sure is. *(Pause)* By the way, Bobby Ray, who's your new starting pitcher?

BAILIFF: Umm . . . uh . . .

JUDGE: Think carefully . . .

BAILIFF: You?

JUDGE: Smart boy.

(They exit.)